Shanta Acharya

What Survives Is The Singing

Indigo Dreams Publishing

First Edition: What Survives Is The Singing
First published in Great Britain in 2020 by:
Indigo Dreams Publishing
24, Forest Houses
Cookworthy Moor
Halwill
Beaworthy
Devon
EX21 5UU

www.indigodreams.co.uk

Shanta Acharya has asserted her right under the Copyright, Designs and Patents Act 1988 to be identified as the author of this work.
© 2020 Shanta Acharya

ISBN 978-1-912876-21-1

British Library Cataloguing in Publication Data. A CIP record for this book can be obtained from the British Library.

This book is sold subject to the condition that it shall not, by way of trade or otherwise, be lent, re-sold, hired out, or otherwise circulated without the author's and publisher's prior consent in any form of binding or cover other than that in which it is published and without a similar condition including this condition being imposed on the subsequent purchaser.

Designed and typeset in Palatino Linotype by Indigo Dreams.
Cover design by Ronnie Goodyer at Indigo Dreams.
Author and cover photos by Dr Sanjay Acharya

Printed and bound in Great Britain by 4edge Ltd.
Papers used by Indigo Dreams are recyclable products made from wood grown in sustainable forests following the guidance of the Forest Stewardship Council.

To my mother –
for her 85th

Life is a spell so exquisite, everything conspires to break it.
~ Emily Dickinson

And we: spectators, always, everywhere,
we face all this, never see beyond it!
It spills from us. We arrange it.
It falls to pieces. We arrange again.
We ourselves fall to pieces.
~ Rainer Maria Rilke

We have a whole world to rearrange.
~ Elizabeth Jennings

In the dark times
Will there also be singing?
Yes, there will be also be singing
About the dark times.
~ Bertolt Brecht

Also by Shanta Acharya

Poetry
Imagine: New and Selected Poems
Dreams That Spell The Light
Shringara
Looking In, Looking Out
Numbering Our Days' Illusions
Not This, Not That

CD
Somewhere, Something: Shanta Acharya reading a selection of her poems

Studies in American Literature
The Influence of Indian Thought on Ralph Waldo Emerson

Fiction
A World Elsewhere

www.shantaacharya.com

CONTENTS

Strange Times	9
Alphabet Of Erasure	10
Can You Hear Our Screams?	12
To Lose Everything	14
Alesha's Confession	16
Ambala	18
Graffiti	20
The Bull Fight	21
The Devil In You	22
Parliament Hill	24
London Eye	25
Homecoming	26
Exile	28
Parallel Lives	29
Days Depart	30
Being Human	32
Possession	33
The Stopped Clock	34
The Umbrella	35
Changing Itself	36
Relationships	37
Continental Drift	38
Friendship	39
Find Your Level	40
Day The Clouds Came Home	41
Woodpecker	42
Spring In Kew Gardens	43
Did You Know?	44
Christmas Gifts	45

Infinity Of Red	46
Self Portrait	48
The Best Is Yet To Be	49
Indian Summer	50
Art Of Ageing	51
Just Wanted	52
Testing The Nation	53
The Art Of Losing	54
Close Encounters	55
Telling Tales	56
Words	57
Less Is More	58
Far From Home	59
Where In This World Does One Find Happiness	60
Not Knowing	61
Why Some People Read Poetry	62
Why Some People Write Poetry	63
In Silence	64
The High Window	65
Not Everything Begins Elsewhere	66
Nothing More Real Than You	67
All You Can Do	68
Just For Today	69
Belonging	70
Home	71
Lethological	72
NOTES	75

What Survives Is The Singing

Strange Times

Strange times are these in which we live –

the falsehoods we are taught, the freedoms we have lost.
Yet humanity never lets go, will not give up the ghost.

It's taken a long time to get here. There's no turning back –
no walls, camps, guards, check-points can prevent

a man on his way home, shopping bags in hand,
stalls a column of tanks as if it were an ordinary thing,

not mankind making a stand, landing on the moon,
planting a flag. They never wanted all that attention –

not the stowaways who died of asphyxiation,
angels who flew for their lives from blazing towers.

The price is always the same, your most precious
possession, your life and dreams, your future

drowned on a beach, face half-buried in sand;
a daughter, brutally violated, dead in your arms.

Not knowing if we can find a way forward,
we stumble on like spirits possessed with sixth sense,

carrying the torch of hope in our hearts,
believing in the darkness of the world –

a crack is all it takes for light to get in,
alter our vision, fire a revolution.

Those who trust know how to dream,
keep faith in things unseen –

the quality of darkness is how it lets us see.

Alphabet Of Erasure

Begins with a bloody Caesarean,
a daughter, perfect almost, yet relegated
to live in the shade if not in oblivion –

crossed out, the way people looking at you
look straight through as if you were invisible,
hidden from your own timeline.

A life spent pursuing other people's dreams,
never realising yours, is self-mutilation,
leaves you diminished, grief-scarred –

no different to being blotted out, bleached
reefs of coral as the earth's treasures disappear
species by species, glacier by glacier.

Every time we lose a language we lose a view
of the world, a slow sclerosis of vision,
not the same as knowing all is illusion.

When barbarians run the city, legislate on art
and beauty in the name of progress and diversity,
rewriting the past with their version of history,

they deny us the gift of exploring the world,
finding our place in it. Truth is nobody's fool –
not a god defaced by humans pretending to speak

nothing but the truth. Before you know it, life's taken
the fork in the road with no signs down the path
of dispossession, nothing you can claim your own –

country, family, faith, freedom, language, memories.
You learn an alphabet of erasure –
amnesia, anorexia, anosmia, aphasia, ataxia –

experience every measure of loss between A and Z
in silence; not a healing, consoling peace where you
find your voice, but the silence of oblivion.

Can You Hear Our Screams?

A chirping bird who ran like a deer
was how her mother described the eight-year-old
whose broken body was found in the bushes.

The day she went missing, the horses returned
without her, giddy with scanning the horizon –
no one heard their screams.

For every girl cracked open like a coconut
in temples, homes, palaces or public spaces,
hundreds more lie buried in basements and attics,

unmarked graves in gardens, forests and fields –
their souls crying out for justice.
Can you hear their screams?

When daughters disappear into earth, water, fire –
discarded at birth with the afterbirth,
flushed into toilets, poured into sewers,

disposed in more ways than you can imagine –
frozen in islands haunted by nightmares,
their prayers turn into screams.

No record exists of how many are kidnapped,
raped, enslaved, starved, burnt, mutilated,
left in bin bags, recycled with the refuse –

not in the national statistics, in gold-plated genealogies,
pages of misogyny in the archives of history.
Can you hear their screams?

The world may be moving closer to the edge
of reckoning as women keep marching
to the roar of injustices trapped in their limbs,

erupting like volcanoes that will no longer
lie dormant or become extinct.
Can you hear our screams?

To Lose Everything

My journey began with a pair of high-heels –
the first thing I saw as she stepped out of her Jaguar.

Slick and poised, the lady called herself Madonna,
always bought something when she visited my stall.
Smoking a pipe she would smile, watch me haggle.

She took me under her wing, spoke of worlds
beyond my dreams – London, Paris, New York, Berlin.

I am from a small village with a handful of houses,
where everybody knows everybody else's business.

As children we never had enough, always wanted more.
Was it so wrong? She gave me gifts – silk stockings,
shoes, scarves, dresses – made me feel special.

Father wanted me to marry a decrepit landlord,
young men these days work and settle abroad.
Life stretched out like an endless dirt road.

One night I left, thinking of making a fresh start.
Some parents give their children roots, others wings.

How would I know there'd be so many men lusting
after the same thing every day, never a day of rest?
The bosses raped us when we slept, even when we bled.

Men are the worst of all animals. And that woman
who traded me into a life I wouldn't curse my enemy
with, what punishment would be right for her?

When the police arrested us, I was not worried.
They sent me to hospital, finally the pain stopped –
but the tempest in my mind kept raging.

Abandonment is a deep, dark ocean of hurt –
none you can trust, none here to offer comfort.

I believed in God, now I don't know what to believe,
know how it feels to lose everything.

Alesha's Confession

Never thought it would come to this –
I'd be the one to bear witness

to the truth about my sister's disappearance,
unveiling the family skeletons, bringing disgrace.

A butterfly with its wings severed, I survived,
trying to forget how free-spirited Shafilea died.

When it was my turn, the arguments were the same –
arranged marriages, family honour and shame,

how we haramzadis preferred besharam western ways.
I was tired of the secrets and lies, the endless alibis.

My parents never thought of their daughters
as rehmat, God's gifts. I felt Shafilea's loneliness,

trapped like a caged bird unable to sing or fly.
Each time she tried she was put back in her prison,

defeated, failing to keep body and soul together.
No one helped – not the police, not social services.

Joking innocently with firangi men, declining
an arranged marriage with a stranger from Pakistan,

planning instead to be a lawyer, find her soulmate,
she wanted to shine, be happy. Was that so wrong?

Could my parents not see things have changed?
My father's no ideal husband. Why the hypocrisy?

Shafilea created such a stink after they dragged
her half-drugged to the airport, drinking bleach the day

they engaged her to a rich, old, contemptible man.
How much pain must one bear before swallowing poison?

She was rushed to hospital, her stomach washed.
But her body was ravaged, her reputation sullied.

Even Allah will not forgive her, the elders proclaimed.
The stain on the family honour kept spreading

as gossip galloped like wild fire through the village.
After they returned my parents were more determined.

That fatal evening mother picked Shafilea from her job,
she was dressed in a skirt, short-sleeved top, stiletto boots.

Tempers flared as Shafilea refused to change her attire,
wear traditional clothes as good Pakistani girls did.

My parents swore revenge as they pinned her down
on the settee, gagging her with a plastic bag.

Struggling to breathe, Shafilea fought back, her limbs
flailing helplessly as father punched her rag-doll body.

The moment we heard mother whisper: Let's finish it here –
a shudder rippled down our spines, a warning loud and clear

to the rest of us as Shafilea gave up the fight;
her life and dreams snuffed out like a candle in the wind.

We watched trembling, huddled upstairs, not a cry escaped
our stunned lips as her body was wrapped in plastic.

How could they do this to their own flesh and blood?
We froze as father drove off into the night.

Ambala

She burst into my room dancing, humming –
a force of nature, her dark skin gleaming,

cleaving me with her beauty's pulse.
I sat face-masked, half-naked, waxing my legs.

Seeing an apology spread large on her face,
holding back the waterfall of words from her lips.

It's alright, I said, thought I'd locked the door.
You can walk into my room any time, she sang –

her statuesque body folding in on itself in a greeting.
My homesickness banished by her peace offering.

Life in a female student dorm was full of surprises,
teaching me how difference makes us human.

The day I knocked on her door, but did not wait
for her regal *Entrée* summoning me in,

I was unprepared to find her in front of a mirror,
peering deep inside herself. Is this a new tantric

yoga posture I was ignorant of? But the stain
on the patterned rug, the agony on her face

told a different story. It hurts, she whispered,
her legs splayed as if giving birth.

I get cramps and back-pain too, I sympathized,
thinking she was suffering from period pains.

No, this is different. A most brutal and unkind cut,
nothing like a male circumcision,

she sighed as I caught sight of her excision –
her wound, her shame, her secret laceration

revealed as she lay writhing on the floor,
unable to mask a life of pain and humiliation.

Can I do anything? I asked, aghast,
thinking there but for the grace of God.

Hold my hand, be my best friend forever.
Apart from the women in my family, no other

person has seen me naked, mutilated.
My ordeal is nothing compared to the horror

of pricking, piercing, cutting, sewing, scraping –
I've survived placing my faith in life, in change.

Her head resting on my lap, our fingers locked,
we stayed there dreaming of a world unmutilated.

Graffiti

Graffiti on walls spew anger, desperation
from the foul mouth of a beast breathing poison.

The tower block is no Banksy exhibition –
guerrilla art in public spaces do not transform lives.

On a hill nearby, female, blue butterflies, maculinea arion,
lay their eggs on buds of thyme. Young larvae born

are nurtured by ants that carry them to underground nests,
where the larvae feed on ant grubs, emerging as butterflies.

We discover particles that travel faster than light.
NASA finds traces of amino acid in the tail of a comet.

Extraterrestrial life may have evolved in space,
come to earth accidentally – the possibilities are immense.

With such a vast intelligence in operation
human beings must thrive no less by comparison.

Yet the last time this young man saw the moonlight
dance in these streets, he watched his friend bleed to death.

He told me it was his turn now. Turn for what?
How was I to know he had been fatally stabbed?

It was hard to see in that unmitigated darkness –
not even a passing car's headlight to reveal

the blood on his clothes, the look on his face.
I sat holding his hand as he lay dying.

The Bull Fight

Man is the cruellest animal. At tragedies, bullfights, and crucifixions he has so far felt best on earth; and when he invented hell for himself, behold, that was his very heaven.   ~ Friedrich Nietzsche, *Thus Spoke Zarathustra*

Men in costumes march ceremoniously into the arena –
a grand entry to the triumphalism of a Paso Doble.

Foot followers draw the bull's attention as he charges in,
disoriented, nostrils flaring, mouth foaming.

No sign of the saint's compassion, just the travesty
of the matador's flourish to display his skill –

wide red cape performing the Verónica, sweeping
close to the bull's face as the saint wiped Christ's.

These wild creatures raised on the vast ranges
of Andalusia are chosen for their tienta, their bravery.

Yet these prize fighters do not stand a chance against
picadores mounted on horses padded, blindfolded, sedated.

Ready with pikes the lancers plunge their weapons
into the bull's neck and hide until he staggers in pain, bleeding.

In the last act the matador with sword in his right hand,
muleta in his left, thrusts the sword into the bull's heart.

Death is not instant, the bull is left standing, a hero heaving,
brightly coloured little flags trembling like medals

on his shoulders – banderillas marking man's inhumanity,
bearing witness to the barbarism of human beings.

A second bull is dragged away, bleeding, from the ring.
The crowd goes wild as the third charges in.

The Devil In You

Once upon a time Good and Evil worked together,
bringing out the best in each other
without sordid stratagems, games of power.

The problem began when a strict division of labour
was introduced without proper procedure –
all in the name of the exploited worker.

Annual appraisals, contracts drove Good to distraction.
While the Gods were debating what to do with Evil,
the Union of Devils was set up by a friendly lawyer.

With a pleasing shape, a Devil-may-care demeanor,
one hand beating the Devil's tattoo, the other dancing
in an empty pocket, the debonair adviser declared:

You can be any kind of Devil you want –
the Attorney-General's or Printer's, but you must
have the Devil in you to succeed in the world.

In pubs, the Devil's Salad was recommended fare,
made of Advocate's tongue, Notary's finger
plus a third secret ingredient selected by the customer.

Some fancied fresh seasoning of vinegar and pepper,
with a choice of dressings: Politician, Journalist, Banker,
Accountant, Estate Agent, Preacher, Doctor, Teacher.

Things haven't been the same in the new world order –
where the Gods built a church, Devils erected a tower.
Not a moment left to man alone with his Maker.

As Good and Evil competed closely against each other,
Devils gathered all the good that belonged to the Gods.
Good folks saw no evil, heard no evil, spoke no evil.

Talk of the Devil, he's sure to appear in disguise –
born of lies is the Devil's compromise.
Talk of an angel and you hear muffled sighs of surprise.

Parliament Hill

Once a Mesolithic camp, now part of a sprawling
heath, home to a flock of flaming flamingos –

the hill attracts modern hunter-gatherers
who arrive armed with iPhones, blankets, hampers.

An ancient site of druidic disputation,
it has not lost its magic, holds a mirror up to us.

Unknown to me its historic name, Traitor's Hill,
where Cavaliers clashed with Roundheads –

a retreat for troops loyal to Parliament.
Here people questioned the King's divine right

to rule, rejected the remorseless rites of power –
eleven years without Parliament, seven without a King.

The Stone of Free Speech, no longer pristine white,
is surrounded by sight-seers and immigrants, debating

the meaning of democracy, justice, freedom, peace –
conjuring heaven on earth with a spell of words.

Call it what you will – civil war, class struggle,
self-realisation? It takes a long time to be human.

At the top of the hill children learn to fly kites,
their feet barely touch the grass glinting in the light.

London Eye

Rising up the arc to the zenith,
twice as fast as a tortoise sprinting,
we move in a transparent capsule,
oblivious of vertigo, surveying
the ancient city's surprised sprawl.
The river passes by naming each building,
old and new, along the embankment.
Glass, steel and concrete façades
shape the landscape. Transcending
the real, dreams rise ghostlike
in the mist of history, announcing
the arrival of the new Londoners,
survivors and inventors, sharing
in their different languages
forgotten stories. Earth and sky
hold on to their secrets, memories
strong enough to overcome suffering,
pain flowering like this metropolis.
At the end of our journey we step out
of the goldfish bowl, get blown
away on a gust of desire,
swept up high, invisible, soaring,
looking down on centuries of struggle,
life hanging on a chance, trusting
to be taken home to *that mighty heart* beating.

Homecoming

In every city I visit, in every cathedral or mosque,
pagoda or temple, gurdwara or synagogue –

in every space en-route to a kind of self-discovery,
I light a candle, offer a prayer.

With every prayer I wish for things –
some material, others not so tangible, for myself

and others I've loved more than you. All through
the hours of my worship I converse with you –

ask why you've withheld the gifts I value most?
Why do you leave me in such uncertainty?

You led me to believe you loved me,
gave me hope fulfilling the smallest desire of mine.

Don't know why I presume you might listen
more carefully to my entreaties in a foreign land?

I am the one on holiday, not you –
such are the limitations of the human mind.

Talking to you, sharing my thoughts, I keep thinking
you will respond, talk to me through your silence.

How can I forget you taught me to accept my need
for you, faith I have sheltered in the storms of doubt?

I try to recall my state of bliss before I was born,
before I demanded my own life separate from you.

If you got hurt you never showed me,
your love kept watch as I lived and got hurt.

How was I to know the consequences of my deeds?
Why did you not protect me from myself?

My loneliness has led me back to where I'd begun.
I've nowhere else to go, don't turn me away
on another journey of self-discovery for I am done.

Exile

A state of mind that grows irrevocably,
seeds of grief sown in a past life, unknowingly –

difficult to be precise of its birth or origin,
bursting into a sapling, sucking all my energy,

spilling out of my skin, putting down roots,
spreading its branches like an ancient banyan tree.

I have been sitting under its shade since,
contemplating the world – nothing is as it seems.

I've stopped wondering if I'm alive,
or merely think I am. Nor do I worry about the sky –

how it feels during that in-between time when my fears
come home before the stars appear playing their symphony.

I can no longer find the map of my dreams.
It used to comfort me, my chador now frayed at its seams.

Everywhere I grow I have to find a world elsewhere,
learn to believe in rebirth, in what life could be.

Living in shadows I learn not to despair
left with an empire of empty promises.

Parallel Lives

Life bears no resemblance to what it might have been,
you simply play a part, an actor on screen,

discover your ideal life exists in a parallel universe,
lived by some stranger with whom you can no longer converse.

What sacrifices are you willing to make to live in your dream?
You offer blood, sweat, tears, the best of yourself, yet they seem

not quite enough to swap one illusion with another.
If lucky you forget your dream, learn to live your

life that bears no resemblance to what it might have been,
you simply play a part, an actor on screen.

Days Depart

Days depart silent, marching solo solemnly.
Turning the key in my door absentmindedly,

I enter. The alarm screams like a banshee.
I feed her with secret codes to keep her happy.

There is a phone message from a stranger.
1471 informs me the caller withheld their number.

As I switch on the radio, plug the kettle for tea,
my smartphone vibrates on the table in ecstasy.

Goes silent the moment I pick up, reports six missed
calls when the postman rings. I fly down the stairs,

but no one's there. A card says he called, I was not in.
Proof I did not imagine hearing the postman ring.

The card informs me I can collect 24 hours later
at the local post office, the item needs my signature.

There's some malarkey outside. I open the door,
thinking I might catch the postman, retrieve my letter.

I find a woman desperately looking for her car
with the children, car keys, mobile phone and shopping.

Did I park in this street or another?
For the life of her she could not remember.

I try to help retrace her journey, hoping
her mind would reconfigure from end to beginning.

Failing to jog the lady's memory, afraid of leaving
her more confused than ever, I offer tea with sympathy.

Spotting the postman's van disappear down the bend
in the road, she gives chase, hands waving, madly.

The microwave beeps, tells me lunch is ready,
takes deep breaths to calm down, remain cool and steady.

I switch on my computer, it springs into action –
a magician conducting numerous tasks with precision,

greets me with the message: *Path cannot be found.*
After all these years not being able to understand

each other, my personal computer and I are destined
for divorce as we prepare for a brave new world.

Later, I settle down to dinner with my favourite thriller.
As if on cue, the landline and mobile phones ring.

When I call back the world is otherwise engaged.
Leaving messages, proving my existence,

I set the alarm for next morning before I go to bed,
switch off and have a long conversation with God.

Being Human

The startling discovery always of the moment –

Keats lost himself in a sparrow,
Whitman found himself in a leaf of grass.

In time everything is transformed –
the deepest ocean floor becomes the roof of the world.

A desert dreaming of its past incarnations
recalls cradling an ancient civilization.

Nothing is, especially the illusion of permanence.
Nature is always in a state of becoming something else.

To know your true self, seekers of enlightenment
have said we must learn to step outside ourselves –

feel the grandeur of the universe,
experience the suffering of all creatures.

Adrift in my world, searching for myself,
I stepped inside myself, met my many selves –

persons I could've been under different circumstances,
accusing me for not creating my chances.

Yet all the time I have been true to myself,
my art a way of seeing without distorting lenses –

the startling discovery always of the moment.

Possession

When I lost something valuable,
I gave it a name, inscribed it on a pebble,

piece of wood, paper, cloth or shell,
placed it in my handbag, let the words settle

in with the rest of my losses defining me –
keys to my anxiety and loneliness,

notebook and pen to record panic attacks,
iPhone, lipstick, comb, cards calling for attention,

tissues folded in cellophanes of adjustment –
carrying on with my chores as if nothing

was the matter, clutching my grief
like a mascot, trying to transcend

that feeling of things missing, life passing,
shrinking, until disappointment rushes in,

weighing me down with further losses,
and my bag too heavy to hold my dreams,

complains this is no way to treasure
hard-earned gifts enriched by dispossession,

awaken to the true nature of being,
no longer be defined by this or that.

The Stopped Clock

There is something reassuring
about Time standing still in this processional

of days – the hands of the clock not moving –
the present, polished and gold-plated

like the carriage clock that stopped for me.
Negotiating my way through a plethora

of things, relinquishing worldly possessions,
hoping to arrive at the essential me,

overwhelmed with that everything-must-go feeling –
shoes, bank statements, suffering.

Instinctively, I hold on to gifts from the past,
unable to let go of memories, my rosary of dreams.

Take away our belongings and we barely survive,
take away our memories and we are nothing.

The Umbrella

Lying under its large appliqué wings –
handcrafted, exotic, bright,
the Pipli garden umbrella
spread like a mythical bird in flight –

my mind weary, seeking emptiness,
I hear a cry of desolation,
a sigh that could only be muted by folding
oneself in like an umbrella.

I remember unfurling my first
parasol like a first kiss – awkward, unsure,
when the wind whooshed in, turning
the metal frame inside out.

Bent, broken, it skulked like a skeleton
behind the door – an extra, never chosen to feature
centre stage, no opportunity to show off its strong,
supple skin, open up, let itself take wings –

be properly forgotten on a bus or train,
venture into other people's homes
like its companion, the walking stick
that went on expeditions far and near.

Even the broom that shared the cupboard
had a life, banishing cobwebs and dust,
making voyages to unexpected places,
sheltering secrets in its bewitched fibers.

They also serve who only stand and wait –
the umbrella never stopped dreaming
of discovering the world, finding its path,
of being most true to itself when serving others.

Changing Itself

from mist and vapour
        to earth and its creatures
                intergalactic water –

the incredible journey
        from before the beginning
                of time, before the spirit moved

upon the face of waters
        making universes
                dividing water from water –

colourless, odourless,
        lacking shape, taste
                complete yet miscible

capable of being anything
        finding its voice with others
                holding infinite possibilities

in a landscape of illusions
        revealing how life flows
                acquiring the essence of things

it touches, taking new identities
        wanting to be changed, mended
                losing itself in everything it encounters

transforming, keeping an open mind
        an unstoppable force of nature
                changing the world by changing itself

Relationships

your first breath   a wild peacock-cry
a clear protest at entering our world

the umbilical cord severed
nurse confirmed   a perfect daughter

the curl of your lips   arch of your eyebrows   all mine
the shape of cells in your blood   our shared DNA

happiness overflowed   my milk dried up
a woman's life is hard   how am I to protect you?

shrine of your immaculate body entrusted in my hands
our eternal exhaustion   common misery

this the moment of renunciation
remembering women in whose footsteps we walk

daughter   mother   grandmother   great-grandmother
linking us all the way back through time

celebrating the journey   memories of places
travelled   together   apart   shared

flowing from the same glacier
head of the soul mountain to a drop in the ocean

tree of life   leaves quivering in the sun
boughs swaying in the rain   invisible sap rising

you tug me back   peering into my eyes
we contemplate each other   ancient enemies   best friends

I barely blinked   yet fifty years have flown
no need to explain the enduring resilience of the connection

we have so much to give   standing there alone
free   ready for flight   not frozen in fear
                            trapped in relationships

Continental Drift
it is so long since my heart has been with yours
						~ E. E. Cummings

You walked into the walled garden of my sacred
courtyard, changing the colour and contour
of our lives, landscapes merging into each other,
making us forget where one ends, the other begins.
Love mints its image everywhere,
stamps its seal, preserves its kingdom,
commanding its citizens to obey its laws
making differences disappear magically.
After the mingling of eyes, lips, bodies,
our separate selves can no longer find their way
back to how they were individually,
like continents long frozen surprised to discover
tigers and wild animals roaming majestically
in the tropical forests of their territories.

Friendship

Like birdsong beginning inside the egg,
a flake of snow dreaming of an iceberg –

the rainbow sky beyond judgment,
one soul dwelling in two bodies,

names safe in each other's mouths,
walking together, sometimes in the dark

in silence more sympathetic than words,
something understood, treasured –

not a duty, just a responsibility gladly undertaken,
a comfortable hand-in-glove feeling.

When the giving grows, the taking goes,
angels let us see the best of what we can be

just as the shimmer of dawn prophesies
the appearance of the Milky Way and a zillion stars –

not following, not leading, just loving
for trying, not blindly, but closing one's eyes

in forgiveness, in prayer, finding the hard times
worth suffering, there being no better love than love

with no object, just being there, unquestioning,
willing to be trusted with everything.

Find Your Level

A slip of a stream sliding
down mountains, gathering
        pace, confidence,
                bouncing up boulders,
disappearing into crevasses,
exploring the landscape of her birth –

the glacier's head where the sun sits smoking
        idly all day long, watching the world –

rehearsing to roll over scree, clay, mud,
        hills and falls, gathering momentum.

If you wish to go fast you must go alone –
        she hums as she skips along.

A river in full spate she surveys
        her tributaries spread across vast plains
swollen by her siblings' strength,
        as they meet, part, and meet again,
powerful currents flowing in symphony.

If you want to go far travel with others –
        they sing in chorus holding hands.

At the confluence cross-currents coexist,
        the waters merge into one mighty river
moving like a matriarch with her family.

The memory of her mother's songs echoes
in her veins as she flows into the sea –

fed by earth and sky, buffeted by fire and air,
learn to overcome loneliness, find your level.

Day The Clouds Came Home

Blowing open doors, ushering the sky in,
drenching us in a spray mist of hope,
a rainbow looking in on our courtyard,
and flowers on their knees, worshipping –

leaving us wondering how some waters
fall, some bend, curve, flow,
rise like incredible angels of hope
while others vanish like ghosts
into the earth, becoming one with the universe.

We were entranced with the miracle of water,
not just the kind that roar in your ears
while flowing silently in your veins,
or the transparent types – dew, sweat, rain,

glistening in the light, a shower of stardust,
not to mention the opaque introversion
of fog, mist, frost and snow –
fresh faced children fingering the fields.

It was the day her waters broke,
her body a reservoir bursting
and a thousand questions came home,
searching for answers, something to do with love –

a promise splashed across the horizon,
turning into tears to brighten the eyes,
holy water to leaven the soul, water that kissed
our lips, leaving us laughing, crying –
in an astonishment of meaning.

Woodpecker

Persistence resonating purpose, passion
reminding us of beings without form –

the unmistakable signature, drum roll
tattoo of bill, beating against bark in rhythm.

Yet nowhere is the wryneck to be seen,
camouflaged in the trees. I am not the only one

walking in Highgate Wood with my face upturned,
eyes scanning branches of trees, April bare,

giddy with birds' nests swaying in the wind
perched precariously high up in the air,

caught in crotches of sturdiest oak and hornbeam.
As the frenzied pecking of the woodpecker fades,

we spot robins, jays, wagtails, starlings
with many a thought that did not come flying.

The sky-calling, whistling, twittering,
cheeping and chirping, cawing and chattering,

the screeching, hooting and trilling –
bird chorus celebrates all that is hidden.

Bluebells sleep buried in earthworks,
dreaming of things tired eyes cannot see.

In the distance a fleeting vision of zygodactyl feet,
profile of a dappled great spotted disappearing.

Spring In Kew Gardens

Under the spell of cherry blossoms,
verging on crimson-maroon to blushing white,

loneliness scatters like particles of dust in light.
I suck the honey of this delicious solitude.

Lifted on the wings of a warbler's song,
a cuckoo's ecstatic call carries me home –

I'm speaking to my mother recovering
from her fall. She calibrates her voice against

the koels' song, full throated, unseen among
the trees in her courtyard. Is it the other way round,

we wonder, birdsong rising in decibels
as noise in cities grows deafeningly loud?

Planes flying over the Royal Botanic Gardens
distract from the peace of ancient trees.

The all-seeing peacocks, their fanned tails quivering
with wild, forlorn calls awaken in me immortal longings,

making it possible to be in two places at once.
I am in Mathura, inside the temple of Krishna,

waiting for darshan. Outside, these proud defenders
of faith and grace teach us to be incorruptible,

discover our inner strength and beauty, display
our true colours as we dance to the music of humanity.

I came into this world with only my shadow,
wake unexpectedly to this rapture of being.

Did You Know?

A tiger doesn't kill because it cares not for
its prey's religion, politics, sexuality or skin colour.

The sea does not rise in a tsunami to teach others a lesson.
A plague kills almost everyone in a village, fire destroys a town.

It's not a war waged by viruses, nor revenge
sought by the elements upon the city's inhabitants.

The sky doesn't send rain and hailstorms, lightning and thunder
for the fun of frightening creatures, see them suffer.

The earth does not shake and crack up because it feels like it.
The wilderness is present everywhere without knowing it.

Snakes do not bite because they are cast as evil in the Bible,
they hiss and attack when threatened like any other animal.

A volcano does not erupt because it is angry with its neighbour,
only when its insides buckle, events it has no control over.

The sun doesn't fake sickness, nor does the moon take a day off work.
The stars do not go on a walkabout, the earth does not go on strike.

Butterflies taste with their feet, crocodiles can't stick their tongues
out, rats laugh when tickled. Giraffes do not sleep much,

fight with their necks and can kick off a lion's head.
Camels smile because they know all the names of God.

A bird doesn't sing because it has an answer –
it sings because it has a song.

Christmas Gifts

The morning sun burst forth excitedly
like a child drawing the curtains on a sea-sky
of cumulus clouds, climbing crazily

over diamonds glinting on snowclad gable
roofs, cajoling me out of bed that I may marvel
at a world gorgeously gift-wrapped –

the scene is pure white, silent lace spread
over sleepy rooftops, smoking chimneys and
TV aerials, camouflaged antlers of trees.

The wind had taken leave for the day,
having departed with its musical tattoo
it so loves to practice on my rickety windows.

Last night I celebrated midnight mass live
from Westminster Cathedral, courtesy of the BBC,
with tidings of joy from the Adventist chorale on ITV –

the wind conducted its own grand ceremony,
beating the drums of fortune on my Victorian glass
bay window touched by a wild, full-moon ecstasy.

Life has taught me to cherish the gifts of time –
Ave Maria. Agnus Dei. Veni Sancte Spiritus.
The afternoon sun offered to unwrap my gifts.

The hours invited me to communion in Highgate Wood
with the squirrels and robins, blackbirds and crows.
Pigeons and dogs greeted each other, not forgetting me.

There were human faces too wrapped in winter.
My neighbours could not stop for me, though the royal trees'
Christmas message was delivered just for my pleasure.

Infinity Of Red

Lips   blushing cheeks   hennaed hands and feet

Desire blazing like autumnal leaves
Maple   honey   amber   russet   scarlet

Colour of magic   passion   purity
Flowers of the gulmohur tree   flame of the forest
Fields of poppies   bouquets of red roses

Crimson ivy   hibiscus   fuchsia   peony
Pomegranate seeds scattering like rubies
Cedar   sandalwood   dogwood   magnolia
Cherry   radish   red cabbage   tomato   chillies

Red button in the Mandarin's cap
Coral   garnet   agate   cornelian
Red cap   revolutionist bohemian
Red tincture   Philosopher's stone   colour of Aries
Judas' hair   Beefeater man   red lattice phrases

Red herring   Red Sea   Red Indian   red line
Red Cross   peace   neutrality   blood bank
HIV   children dying of AIDS   blood diamonds
Red in heraldry   Red Devils   fortitude   endurance
Red light   red flag   danger signal
Red light district   brothel   Cupid   Devil

Red blooded man   anaemic woman
Low haemoglobin   iron   menses
Red rag   bullfight   red cape   Little Red Riding Hood
Red dragon   red ants   crabs   lobsters   scorpions
Red flags   countries in the red   bound in red tape
Red box of the Chancellor of the Exchequer
Caught red handed   red faced like a monkey

Shades of red in earth   sky   sunrise   sunset
Red planet   Mars   volcano   lava
Forest fires   smouldering embers   logs in the hearth
Christmas   gifts wrapped in red tinsel   sprigs of holly
Red berries   red snow   coral reefs   Red Sea
Red squirrel   red kite   red fox   Red Sox
Redbrick   Terracotta Army   Red City   red turbans
Stockings   suspenders   redneck City traders

Painting the town red   Valentine's Day   red nose day
Campari   port   red wine   beer   tea   Bloody Mary
Cinnamon   turmeric   Chilli red curry   tandoori
Mango   papaya   watermelon   strawberry
Gulab jamun   gajjar halwa   jalebi   amruti
Red caviar   roasted meat   red Cuban cigars
Telephone booths   post boxes   London buses
Deities in red quelling demons   deities healing
Christ on the Cross   bleeding heart   Bloody Sunday

Mary in maroon-red and blue   *The Annunciation*
Marilyn Monroe   *Niagara*   Julia Roberts   *Pretty Woman*
Red carpet   royal receptions   red shoes   red Ferraris
Indian weddings   red Benarasi silk saris
Vermillion on the bride's forehead   red eyes   love bites
Red bangles   *sankha*   blood on the sheets
Red letter day   celebrations   blood on the streets
Sadhus in saffron robes   rudraksha beads   prayer flags
Love letters written in blood   bruises   wounds
A newborn child wrapped in its amniotic fluid crying

Self Portrait

There's someone in the mirror smiling at me,
the image is mine but who is that person?

Looking at a photo of me looking years younger,
standing beside the mirror I see incarnations of myself –

the stranger in the mirror, the person in the photo,
both looking at me. I am many.

The moment I become the person I want to be,
I'm somebody else. I ask myself who am *I*
when I say – *I* am, *I* love, *I* believe?

I ask the people who know me,
including my enemies, my best friends, about this *I*.

Opinions vary widely, the centre cannot hold,
once revealed they take wings, irrevocably.

The sketches reflect the character of the individual
drafter, not even a passing glimmer of me –

imagine finding yourself in an exhibition
where none of your portraits resemble you.

Not this, not this – that is not me, *I* whisper
to the gallery, waiting for a reckoning.

Becoming different things to different people,
I disappear in shadows, dissolve like a dream.

Fragile as a jigsaw puzzle, the canvasses crumble
with vital tessellating pieces missing, each segment

an unfathomable life that belongs only to me –
an opportunity to weigh myself in the balance,

not find myself wanting, an eternity to make things
right, discover what manner of human I have been.

The Best Is Yet To Be

Weaving the years into an uncommon yarn,
I walk through walls, invisible, without a bone

in my body, gathering days like blessings,
observing the world as never before.

Grandmother, mother, wife, daughter, sister, lover, whore –
words that defined us changing like litmus paper.

No longer Charlie's Angel, I am a supreme deity –
not Cinderella, Sleeping Beauty, Savitri, Sita or Draupadi.

Takes a lifetime to be oneself, translate the world
in one's own language. Creativity does not

come easily, cannot be bought or sold.
It's a skill to be honed, a gift to be earned.

After years of perfecting my creations,
expecting nothing, ready to relinquish everything,

learning the language of the universe,
realising love is when giving feels like receiving,

I encounter a sky bright with shooting stars,
swirling auroras in a trance, dancing.

Indian Summer

The vulnerability of a full blown rose raging
in my body, I wake in a sweat – flushed, shattered.

Is this nature's way of teaching Time's intransigence,
this body no more a still life portrait, perfect bowl of fruit?

There is nothing comforting about the clock ticking away,
just the obscenity of the eternally swinging pendulum.

Kicking off the covers, I try to cool down,
take deep breaths, apply cold cream on my face,

hands, body – magic potion to ward off nightmares.
I wait for the fever to disappear. The Indian summer

of my body, warm like freshly baked bread –
no lover within the cover, only a blood-sucking mosquito, dead.

Picture of dews on rose buds, invisible writing on the wall,
that you-cannot-trust-anyone-not-even-God feeling,

banishing sleep from every cell in my body
in the middle of the darkest hour of the night.

Age is ultimately the triumph of matter over mind,
revenge for the idealistic delusions of youth.

Must change painting, I make a mental note, adding drops
of avena sativa to half a cup of water and drink.

Gazing upon the blasted rose buds I switch off the lights,
draw the duvet over my head, imagine winters in the Himalayas.

Art Of Ageing

Growing old gracefully is no simple task,
the trick is to relax, take off your mask.
Stop worrying about things you have no control over.
Sleep as much as you want. When you wake,
stay in bed savouring the hours.
No point in rushing out, things will take care
of themselves as they have for centuries.
Switch off the radio or TV the moment you find
it neither educational nor entertaining,
unless cursing and shouting prove therapeutic.
Avoid social media, do not answer the phone
to cold callers with ghastly recorded voices
threatening to cut off your connection.
No point in not revelling in a world of your own.
Let the young and foolish fume and rage,
preserve your energy for life's endless surprises.
Practise your Mona Lisa smile when you are out
and about. At home, laugh as much as you please,
as loud as you can, with or without anyone.
Making faces at yourself in front of a mirror
can get rid of those wrinkles and frown lines.
Remember to chuckle when you are disappointed,
say confidently: A – E – I – DON'T – O – U anything!
When you pray no point in thanking the Lord
for all the things He hasn't done, or repenting
for the things you have. If you haven't been heard
in all these years, do not take it personally.
There may or may not be a reason for everything.
Keep an open mind, but don't be afraid to hold on
to what you believe. Develop a sense of the absurd.
Wear your heart on your sleeve if you please,
but don't just stick to purple. Try all the colours
that make you swing; mix and match, do all the things
you never dared, be the centre of your world.

Just Wanted

Just wanted to say... I ....

You interrupted me with a wave
of your hand, as if to say:

You don't have to say it, yet...
We barely know each other, we've only just met.

Which you did! And I said:
What's wrong with saying it to friends?

To which you responded, incredulously:
You say it to all your friends?

Yes, I say it to all my friends –

You do? Perhaps, you don't mean it?
I mean... not in the same way?

Of course, I mean it; why else say it?

Well, what can I say –
thought things between us were special?

Yes, they are; that's why I want to say it.

Say it as if you mean it.

I'll do my best, I said, flushing my winter
throat with mulled wine and Xmas cheer –

Here's wishing you a very Happy New Year!

Testing The Nation

If the Hundred Years' War lasted a hundred and sixteen,
and the October Revolution took place in November,

if Chinese gooseberries are from New Zealand
and Panama hats from Ecuador,

if cat gut is made from the bowels of sheep and other
animals, and camel's hair brush from squirrel fur,

if the Canary Islands were named after dogs
and King George VI's first name was Albert,

if English muffins are not from England,
nor French fries from France –

then waht is rong if r chilren
canot reed or rite, lak comun sens,
tink egs do not gro in Grate Britun
and potatos r milkt from caus?

The Art Of Losing
(With acknowledgement to Elizabeth Bishop)

The art of losing isn't hard to master –
life's subtle game of snakes and ladders is meant
to make you stronger, which is no disaster.

Remaining in office but not in power,
your majority lost in Parliament –
the art of losing isn't hard to master.

Then practice losing farther, losing faster –
Achilles heel of the Withdrawal Agreement,
the Irish border, promising disaster.

Losing support from every corner; vaster
realms lost before, empires – this continent
of humiliation isn't hard to master.

Deal, no-deal, this kingdom-for-a-deal bluster,
touting rigged lottery tickets incumbent
on fake gods, this Brexit is no disaster.

Losing all I believed in is a measure
of my fall from grace. Is it not evident
the art of losing's not too hard to master –
kissing snakes, kicking ladders, quelle disaster!

Close Encounters

Turning away from a whiff of his Jaguar
Eau-de-toilette stirred in sweat, I hold my breath,
feign to read the words half eclipsed by his head
when the carriage does a jig, drawing us cheek-
to-cheek – the *Nation's Favourite Poems*
spread between us like filler in sandwich.
Reconfigured in a superfast blind date,
the writing on the wall now winks with such
abandon that close to asphyxiation
as Saharan ash and Iberian dust paint
London into an apocalyptic saffron,
claustrophobia rising, I head for the exit,
can't help thinking of the smart Dover sole
that stunned the world with its kamikaze kiss.

Telling Tales

Lean on truth not lies, my mother once said
when she overheard us telling tales,
each more fantastic than the other.

Think twice before you say nothing –
my father once said when words flew
out of my mouth for which I paid dearly.

Time is the best storyteller, both my parents said
when words became my *metier*, and I spent
my days eating, breathing, dreaming words.

Words

They wake you up, your bed of words,
without warning – wild, wicked words, whirling
through waves of astonishment,
a world-without-end ecstasy – quickening
the pulse of your being, breathing life
into things, making the ordinary extraordinary,
and you feel the exhilaration of walking
in a field of light gifted with insight,
life's contradictions temporarily reconciled,
imagine your creations rising like suns
on the shores of continents of strangers,
networks of neurons connecting the universe.
The joy is all yours, nothing's the same anymore –
not the past, present, not even the future.

Less Is More

Is more or less the case.
A true poet will swear by such a hypothesis –

weed out adjectives, embrace
the energy of verbs, the wholesomeness

of nouns. Even homeopathy teaches
us the power of diluted doses.

More exercise and eating less
are paths to health and physical grace.

We do not need experts to tell us
the world's resources are scarce,

or that if we consumed less
the earth might be a better place?

Far From Home
(For Naomi Shihab Nye)

Dancing with words on a page rich with meaning
is a kind of going home, floating free –

like running fast enough, leaving your loneliness
panting behind at the bottom of the hill

as you disappear into an ancient wood
echoing with chorus of birdsong that has never known

loneliness. The sighs of hedges, the swoon of honeysuckle
feed you even when you cannot imagine their hopes

tapping up the pavement, whispering what they wish for
when they go far from home.

Where In This World Does One Find Happiness
(After Li Po)

– dreaming of worlds other than the one we live in?
Like moths to flames we are drawn to illusion.

If happiness is knowing your limitations,
begin with identifying your strengths –

know yourself, your only treasure,
learn to protect it from others.

When asked a word do not offer the *Mahabharata*
containing thousands of universes –

*Nothing there could be in any way diminished
nor, to what is there, could anything be added,*

*what is here may be found elsewhere,
but what is not here is found nowhere else.*

All the things of this world are, have always been.
May the worlds we make, make harmony.

Is poetry so bitter, bitter the company of poets,
a jungle consuming itself like a raging fire?

Like moths to flames we are drawn to illusion,
dreaming of worlds other than the one we live in.

Not Knowing
The poet does not write what he knows but what he does not know…
          ~ W.S. Graham

Using language as a pitchfork,
not knowing what you don't know
is a gift: what you know
a speck of dust barely visible in the fog.

With or without an architecture of its own –
hieroglyphs on a page may be child's play,
keeping you out of trouble –
but you cannot know what you don't know.

When trouble comes riding on its chariot
of erasure, expels you from the magic circle
for doubting the emperor's new clothes,
remember the world is as numinous as words.

If you take the risk of roaming far from home,
keep faith in what you don't know –
living on silence is harder than you know.

And if *you hear somebody knocking
on the other side of words*, be prepared
for *the beast in the space* hungry for your love.

Knowing how to live or die without a measure
of words saves you from not knowing if words
make a difference, refract the light of the universe,
provide a reason for our being here.

Why Some People Read Poetry
(After W. S. Merwin)

Because you know already if you didn't
you would have to make that appointment
which means you would have to spend a lot
of time talking, not to mention money you do not
have, to someone who will not be listening
or listening without hearing, maybe hearing
without understanding, and what good would
that do to you if you were not even heard
like that mad man shouting across the road
stumbling then not moving after falling: God
knows it is past midnight, you are driving fast
alone to get home then hitting something, lost
in a strange part of town looking for help, mugged
by some crazy buggers who leave you for dead.

Why Some People Write Poetry

Because you know already if you didn't
you'd be lost when the world is too much with us –
no more unacknowledged legislators, just ordinaries
living at the margins – the freedom may be exhilarating,
it's no panacea for the unintelligibility of the universe;
poems are pilgrim souls, lost alphabets fallen off signs
like words culled from dictionaries, seeking to find a niche
in the world, a space inviolable, keeping at bay that sense
of uncertainty, futility, each according to his measure –
a lover conjuring possibilities of union, a mystic
dancing within an arrangement of words, a traveller
slouching home, coat heavy with stories slung
over the shoulder, humming to the sleep of a million
dreams, keeping warm a child you've promised a home.

In Silence

When fate deals you a losing hand, play in silence.
Luck favours those who mend themselves in silence.

Remember precious lessons learnt in defeat –
pearls of experience purchased in silence.

A game of chance, nothing in this world is real,
our stories shadows passing in silence.

Be the flame of a candle to what blows you –
life is the greatest gift bestowed in silence.

Days are restless until your heart finds a home,
a sky where you can be yourself in silence.

Earth's grand gardens may beckon you in your dreams,
love's a patch of green that flowers in silence –

a shade that shelters you in times of crises,
a place you keep returning to in silence.

To hold, be held the Beloved eternal –
believe in the splendour of grace in silence.

Silence is the keeper of keys to secrets –
Shantih that passes understanding in silence.

The High Window

An act of kindness never goes unnoticed,
the praise of prayer-wheels they say is heard from
                              the high window.

In life's intricate game of snakes and ladders,
winner takes it all, face against the sun framed in
                              the high window.

When moonshine dances on stained sun-kissed glass,
lovers like fire flies flock to worship at
                              the high window.

Long as you keep your rainbow window open,
shafts of light will stream in like helping hands through
                              the high window.

Hearts like mirrors can shatter hearing music.
One day songs will soar, flooding the gods, out of
                              the high window –

my words one with the hum of the universe,
and the endless horizon glowing beyond
                              the high window.

Not Everything Begins Elsewhere

Some things start right here
within the unfathomable heart of desire,

irritant in oyster maturing into priceless pearl.
Now close your eyes, let your inner universe unfurl.

Cast aside all doubt of your ability to soldier on,
knowing failure has as many faces as stars in heaven.

Celebrities arrive disguised like masked guests at a ball
dancing in a hall of mirrors, holding you in thrall.

In the clear light of day, stripped naked,
success appears arbitrary, undeserved.

Greatness comes not from trying to please others,
nor does it come trailing clouds of glory blinding us.

It lives among us unnoticed, goes about its business
like sap flowing with the iridescence of consciousness.

Nothing More Real Than You

The world may appear to be your oyster,
remember it is not yours to keep or conquer.

You may never discover why you are here,
if you have a special place in the universe.

There may be planets inhabited by creatures
infinitely more intelligent and conscious than us.

By the time you figure out most things you believed
in are flawed, half a century will have disappeared.

Things change faster than you can imagine,
leaving you running in the same spot quick as you can.

No point in prising open your priceless treasure
with a sword, nothing worth having is won by force.

Build therefore your own world. If you start early
you might learn to make a home of it eventually.

Explore the vast continents of yourself –
nothing in this world is real, nothing more real than you.

All You Can Do

Here's your thunder stolen by others,
your losses, ships that never return.

Here's your life passing slowly by,
your body of song promising all it can do.

Here's your heart reaching out to others,
your thoughts fresh rays of sun.

Here's your dream scattered across the sky,
falling stars not knowing what they can do.

Here's hope, gold at the edge of the rainbow,
casting a spell on us as we go.

Here's your fear walking in front of you,
thinking there is nothing you can do.

Here's my hand, place yours in mine,
I'll show you the world is yours.

Here's your true love waiting for you,
your tree of life, radiant in bloom.

Here's what you do, what you can do,
it's your future, make of it what you will –

Here's life in all its squalor and splendor,
here's your world and all you can do.

Just For Today

Just for today I will not squander
my time on things of importance or of no importance.

Such decisions carry the illusion of grandeur,
of being the chosen one, placed in a position of power.

One thing leads to another, a sigh turns into a hurricane.
Years later you look back at lives not lived, times gone.

Just for this morning I will let everything be
as it is, knowing nothing in this world is just or true.

I'll stop worrying about things I don't have and what I do.
I will not hanker after eternity or God's eye view.

Just for this hour I'll fly free trusting my instincts,
let imagination steer, steadying me with wings.

Just for this moment I'll be everything and nothing,
be one with the universe, let it open my eyes.

Belonging

To be touched with tenderness,
the curve of your thoughts explored,

shapes they sing in, syllables uttered,
meanings inhaled the way elephants

smell water from a distance.
If only words were licked, turned over,

nuzzled as a matriarch might linger
on the bare bones of an ancestor

lost in a deep, long meditation on a half-
recognised kingdom, every desire a covenant,

when the herd stop to mourn one of their own,
scan the horizon lit by distant flashings

from the past, reading the land as they rumble
on with their journey to a new home.

Only she with the majestic tusks pauses
to taste sorrow, celebrate the chance encounter,

stroking, twirling, twisting, feeling,
her sensitive trunk caressing the carcass

as a blind person memorises a face,
touching, smelling, kissing, holding

on to memories that travel from bone to bone
like words from mouth to mouth.

Home

Home is not a country or postcode,
more a state of mind, keeper of the map of my world –

offering a hint of the distance between myself
and the silence out there, the way life reaches

for light, and rays leaning like ladders against the sky
invest my journey with meaning.

The universe never seems to tire of change,
making itself new, daring me to the challenge.

Time holds my life up against the light,
a tapestry, tattered though richly embroidered –

leaving me with a fresh measure of myself.
No longer sure of anything – even the hands

of my grandfather clock run faster beneath the dust
with each passing season – my body conspires

to slow me down, show me things I've never seen
though they've always been there, camouflaged.

After all this time to be none the wiser
about one's purpose for being here

is a paradox of many worlds –
the ability to be dead and alive until observed.

Living in doubt and darkness is human,
what redeems is the seeing and being seen.

Lethological

Lying in corpse pose, blank as an empty page,
I reach for words on the tip of my tongue –

but words will not stay still, be expected to appear like a saviour at a time of profound crisis, leaving me with the intolerable struggle with memory and meaning

moving through the scanner my body lights
up in a scrum of pain, building images

of abandoned Rohingya villages, women raped, children slaughtered – refugees fleeing from one disaster to another, surpassing the plight of Syrians, Yemenis, Iraqis, Afghanis

like slices of a loaf of bread of each organ,
coloured spectrum of stories on a CT-scan –

how does one survive at the outliers of the human curve where the price is always one's most treasured possession?

virtual libraries stacked with contrasting
columns of formularies, offering

Time's scroll of suffering in a chorus of pain ascending to a stillness – centuries of prayers for justice when darkness descends and the scream sighs 'I am existence'

drafts of the estates of my exhaustion,
maps of my body's imperfection –

an eclipse transforms London into an apocalyptic saffron – someone calls it the end of the world. The eclipse passes and we are bathed in the light of the Big Bang

un-X-rayed the tempest swelling in my mind,
spasms of hurt bordering on ecstasy –

nothing in this world is free, you've paid for it or you will – there's only one earth, we destroy it at our peril. Eating plastic is not an option, nor surviving in sub-human conditions

the way waves of energy dance at the edges
of tiredness, the way autumn colours

where does the world's hate come from – being human must have something to do with love, and love with giving, understanding, compassion?

seize the day before the grey-white-evergreen
flag of winter hoists itself –

the simplest way to corrupt someone is to bestow them with power – fame, success, wealth and power mesmerising as a cuttlefish to its prey

before I lose track of myself, a witch dragging her pain,
splintering down the spine, commanding me

stop listening to the news – is it even real – what was gossip is now headline story; as moths to flames the human race is drawn to self-annihilation

to obey, else rue the day I stopped listening
to my body now branded with the world's

truth is neither the rising sun that banishes the morning mist nor the delicate mist vanishing under its common gaze

suffering, wiser than the experts who probe
my insides for signs of malaise, failing

the gods to themselves keep Justice, humans hold on to Hope – but when gods are forgotten and defaced, what hope is there for us?

to diagnose the cause of my body's grieving,
mysterious bleeding, her pain a moving wall of wings –

bearing witness to the barbarism of human beings, I cannot help wondering if man is the lowest of all animals, the opposite must also be true

my mind randomly recalls scenes from a TV programme of a super orgasmic woman writhing with pleasure inside an MRI scanner

brains exploding with oxytocin spread love, create a circle of trust, excluding others from its largesse – if scientists are right why are so many women killed by their partners?

as the anaesthesia wears off, it dawns on me
that pain is also a way into the mystery of being –

at home in uncertainties, mysteries, doubts, without any irritable reaching after fact and reason – maybe for this world to exist God must too…

and my heart enlarged with letting the universe in,
beats with the arrhythmic exultation of being alive.

NOTES

Epigraphs
Emily Dickinson, *The Life and Letters of Emily Dickinson*, edited by Martha Dickinson Bianchi (Biblo & Tannen Booksellers & Publishers, 1972).

Rainer Maria Rilke, *Duino Elegies*, translated by Martyn Crucefix (Enitharmon Press, 2008).

Elizabeth Jennings' 'Attempted Suicides', *The Collected Poems*, edited by Emma Mason (Carcanet Press, 2012).

Bertolt Brecht, motto to *Svendborg Poems*, 1939, *Bertolt Brecht: Poems 1913-1956*, edited by John Willett and Ralph Manheim (Eyre Methuen, 1976).

Strange Times: The first line is a quote from Plato: 'Strange times are these in which we live when old and young are taught falsehoods in school. And the person that dares to tell the truth is called at once a lunatic and fool.' Lines six and seven refer to the iconic 'Tank Man' who protested during the demonstrations in Tiananmen Square on 5 June 1989. The last line, 'The quality of darkness is how it lets us see' echoes Adrienne Rich's 'The beauty of darkness/ is how it lets you see' and William Shakespeare's 'The quality of mercy…' Reference is also made to a Leonard Cohen line: 'There is a crack in everything, that's how the light gets in'.

Can You Hear Our Screams?: On 10 January 2018, an eight year old girl, Asifa Bano, went missing in Indian administered Kashmir. She belonged to a community of Muslim nomadic shepherds called Gujjars who crisscross the Himalayas with their herds of goats, buffaloes, horses. Her brutal rape and murder, the discovery of her body a week later, brought into focus not just the fault lines between Hindu-majority Jammu and the Muslim-majority Kashmir, but also the culture of sexual violence against females in India and other parts of the world. Preference for boys in India and China resulted in a massive programme of abortion of girls. In several African countries, female genital mutilation is common. Girls are consistently the victims of infanticide, sexual violence, honour killings; poorer access to nutrition, education, medical care, etc. is widely prevalent. Even in developed countries, violence against women is endemic. No data exists to indicate the kinds of abuse that girls/women experience on a daily basis, globally.

Alesha's Confession: Poem based on the honour killing of Shafilea Iftikhar Ahmed by her parents in Warrington, Cheshire, United Kingdom, on 11 September 2003. It was her younger sister, Alesha, whose confession lead to the arrest and conviction of their parents. On 6 October 2016, legislation was passed by the government in Pakistan to make honour-killing a crime.

Ambala: An African girl's name meaning scar.

London Eye: The phrase, *'that mighty heart'* is from William Wordsworth's *'Composed Upon Westminster Bridge, September 3, 1803'*.

Possession: The last line refers to the Hindu concept of divinity as *'neti, neti,'* translating to 'not this, not that,' referring to the idea that the Divine is limitless, beyond definition.

The Umbrella: *They also serve who only stand and wait* – is the last line of John Milton's sonnet 'When I Consider How My Light Is Spent'.

Friendship: The first line *'Like birdsong beginning inside the egg'* is from Rumi.

Testing The Nation: The last stanza is based on answers given by children in a London primary school when asked where eggs and potatoes came from.

The Art Of Losing: The 'Withdrawal Agreement' refers to the draft Withdrawal Agreement Bill of 19 March 2018 which contained agreed legal text for the implementation period, citizens' rights, and the financial settlement, as well as a significant number of other articles in the terms for the departure of the United Kingdom from the European Union, which has been named 'Brexit'. This bill was rejected thrice by Parliament, leading to the departure of Prime Minister, Theresa May.

Close Encounters: The poem refers to a news item about an angler who kissed a Dover sole in celebration of his catch when the six-inch fish wriggled out of his hand and jumped into his mouth. The 28-year-old stopped breathing and suffered a cardiac arrest. Paramedics removed the fish with forceps in an ambulance: http://www.bbc.co.uk/news/uk-england-dorset-41598493. The writing on the wall refers to 'Poems on the Underground' in London. The Nation's Favourite Poems is an anthology published by the BBC of the UK's favourite poems.

Where In This World Does One Find Happiness: Lines by Li Po are from *Bright Moon, White Clouds: Selected Poems of Li Po* edited and translated by J.P. Seaton (Shambala Publications, Boston and London: 2012). Reference to the *Mahabharata* in the poem 'Song for Seng Ka' is unacknowledged by Li Po or by J.P. Seaton in his notes to the poem. For those familiar with the *Mahabharata* the reference is unmistakable: 'Nothing there could in any way be diminished, nor to what is there, could anything be added.' Other lines quoted from Li Po's work include 'Conceal yourself, your only treasure'; 'All the things of this world are, and have always been'; and 'Is poetry so bitter, so bitter, my friend?' The lines *'what is here may be found elsewhere, /*

but what is not here is found nowhere else' is from the *Mahabharata*. I have used Wendy Donegir's translation in her 'Foreword' to *Mahabharata: A Modern Retelling* by Carole Satyamurti (W.W. Norton & Company, New York/ London 2015).

Not Knowing: Words in italics are by W.S. Graham.

Why Some People Write Poetry: The phrase 'the world is too much with us' is the title of a sonnet by William Wordsworth. 'Unacknowledged legislators' refers to "A Defence of Poetry" an essay by Percy Bysshe Shelley, containing Shelley's famous claim that 'poets are the unacknowledged legislators of the world'.

In Silence: *'Silence is the keeper of keys to secrets'* from "Things" by Agha Shahid Ali, *Call Me Ishmael Tonight* (W.W. Norton & Company, New York/ London: 2003). *'Shantih'* in Sanskrit means peace.

ACKNOWLEDGEMENTS

My thanks to the editors of the following publications in which several of these poems, or earlier versions, first appeared:

Words and Worlds Magazine (Austria); *Bengal Lights* (Bangladesh); *The Dance of the Peacock: An Anthology of English Poetry from India* (Canada); *World Poetry Yearbook 2014 and 2015* (China); *A World Assembly of Poets: Contemporary Poems, Das Literarisch, Guftugu/Indian Cultural Forum, 100 Great Poems For Children, Illuminati: A Transnational Journal of Literature, Language and Culture Studies, Impressions, Indian English Women Poets, Indian Literature, Journal of the Poetry Society, Kavya Bharati, Lakeview International Journal of Literature and Arts, Muse India, Pragati's English Journal, The HarperCollins Book of English Poetry, The Little Magazine, To Catch A Poem: An Anthology for Young People, Re-Markings, Roots and Wings: An Anthology of Indian Women Writing In English, Suvarnarekha: An Anthology of Indian Women Poets Writing in English, The Punch Magazine, Wings Over The Mahanadi: Eight Odia-English Poets* (India); *Acumen, Agenda, And Other Poems, ARTEMIspoetry, Confluence, Diversifly: Poetry and Art on Britain's Urban Birds, Envoi, Exiled Ink, Eyewear, For the Silent: An Anthology to aid the work of the League Against Cruel Sports, Journal of Postcolonial Writing, London Grip, Magma, Message in a Bottle, Morphrog, New Hope International, Orbis: Quarterly International Literary Journal, Poetry Nottingham International, South Bank Poetry, Stand, The Chronicles of Eve, The Editor: An Anthology for Patricia Oxley, The Missing Slate, The Poetry Shed, The New European, The New Writer, The Spectator, Thumbscrew, Under the Radar, Word Masala Award Winners 2015: An Anthology* (UK); *Fulcrum: An annual of poetry and aesthetics, Life and Legends – From the Cradle of Civilization: Contemporary Indian Poetry, Poetry Pacific, Snowy Egret, The Literary Review* (USA).

My thanks and gratitude to Ronnie Goodyer and Dawn Bauling of Indigo Dreams Publishing.

Special thanks to my brother, Sanjay, for the cover photograph. Without the support of my family and friends none of this would have been possible.

Indigo Dreams Publishing Ltd
24, Forest Houses
Cookworthy Moor
Halwill
Beaworthy
Devon
EX21 5UU
www.indigodreams.co.uk